PAU[illegible]OKSON

For Karen
who remembers Pete Duel
+ Slade!
All the best
Paul [illegible]

42

First published : August 2003
by A Twist In The Tale
P.O. Box 25, Retford, Notts, DN22 6SR
ISBN 1 874335 12 5

Cover by Sally Cookson

Typesetting and printing by :
Herbert Robinson, Elizabeth Court,
Manners Industrial Estate, Ilkeston, Derbyshire.
Tel : 01159 442063

The poems in this book are dedicated
to all of my family and friends
— after all, you are the ones who inspires them.

Thanks,

Paul

An introduction of sorts ...

Hiya and welcome to "42" …

Why 42? Well, I'm now 42 years old, which is 2 x 21, it's 25 years since I (self) published my first collection of poems (can it really be that long?), I once did a book called *Over 21 And Still Into Noddy*, it's Greenbelt Festival's 30th anniversary and I've been performing there for 25 of the 26 years I've been going … and for some reason all these numbers fit together somehow. Plus, there's 42 poems.

These poems represent where I am now I suppose, although I haven't included any children's poems as such. For the last fourteen years I've worked as a poet, mostly in schools and have edited numerous collections and anthologies for children so there's plenty of them out there – check the Macmillan and Lion lists if you're interested. These poems however, haven't found homes yet, which is why they're here.

Some of them are culled from other themed collections – *The Glam Rock Football Love Poems / Still Waiting For My Blue Peter Badge* – childhood and growing up poems. Then there's *Something About Guitars* – a collection inspired by rock and roll and such like. Plus there's a miscellaneous selection and plenty of poems about those people who've inspired and interested me, so if there's any interested commissioning editors out there who want a poetry book that's accessible …

Anyway, 42 is where I am now and for those who've been part of this journey for many years – many, many thanks, your company and encouragement is very much appreciated. However, I'm afraid there's more to come, I can't let you off the hook just yet, so stick around please. Here's to the next 21, 25, 42 or whatever.

Yours,

Paul
August 2003

42

Contents

The First Poem Of The Day

is usually not the best,
muddled and cluttered, no real clarity or direction,
just sort of me arranging and rearranging my thoughts
- a sort of poetic desk clearing,
if you can have such thing as a poetic desk.
I wouldn't be averse to such a thing but nothing much
actually rhymes with desk
... apart from *burlesque, grotesque, statuesque, picturesque,*
arabesque, Romanesque, sculpturesque, humouresque,
Moresque and Junoesque.
I have no idea what the last two are
but I suppose a desk could be all of the others ...
a burlesque desk that's picturesque
grotesquely statuesque
arabesque and sculpturesque ...
but I've lost interest already.
Maybe you could have *best* at a push
if you slurred it and said it fast
(and *fast* would be *fest* if you were from the posher Home Counties)
but it's only a half rhyme and they don't really count.

Being a first poem
it may go off at tangents
wondering whether to cover such areas as
childhood memories (done loads like that but always like them),
family and friends (ditto),
God, Slade and Everton (ditto, but never all three in the same poem,
often two but never all three,
maybe that's a challenge, maybe it is,
but not today.)

It's too early for philosophy and politics, life and death.
I'm not in the mood for love
- actually I am but my wife is out.
Dexterous puns and witty worthy wordplay
are too much like hard work at this hour,
especially combined with rhyming couplets
and not much rhymes with *couplet* either.

Far too long for a haiku
although I could go
back and start to count

Seventeen sylla-
bles and break it all up in
neat little verses

but I can't be bothered.

Cinquains never tempt me
I can't spell *Acrostic*
Limericks are too restricting
I'm rubbish at villanelles
And I've never been able to complete a sonnet anyway.

I don't write about flowers and trees
and I can't make up my mind
whether I want profundity or humour
or possibly both,
or maybe neither -
as is likely with a poem like this.

I always want to end up on an upbeat note
but this being the first poem of the day
I can't think of an original one
and the best thing I can offer
is a pun based joke a seven year old girl told me
during a recent school visit
(I don't usually let children tell jokes
as all the lads invariably end up telling mucky ones
but she looked sweet and innocent...)
Anyway, the joke, the big finish,
what big Finnish - Sammi Hyppia,
he's a big Fin, a big Finnish footballer
who plays for Liverpool but that's not the joke ...

Q. What's the difference between roast beef and pea soup ?
I don't know, what is the difference between roast beef and pea soup?
A. Most people can roast beef, but not many people can pea soup.

Don't worry if you don't get it at first, you will,
plus I bet it's the one thing from the poem that you remember
and tell to someone else tomorrow.

Pee soup, Geddit now?

You Are The One That This Poem Is For

You are my constant, my straight and my narrow
You are my leveller, you are my truth
You do the things that I take for granted
You are the one that I come home to

You are my constant, the one never changing
You are my foundation, unshakeable, true
You are the one who makes all things possible
I could not be me if you were not you

You are my constant, friend and companion
You are my love, my lover and more
The one who upholds me, the one who enfolds me
You are the one that I write this poem for

A Crocodile Thermometer And An Orange Uttan

It's still there
on a window sill,
used to be on the old fireplace hearth.

It's always been somewhere,
the crocodile thermometer,
red line and numbers on its back.

I can't remember how
but the tail got broken at the end,
glued together ever since, you can see the join.

A grey short pocket sized present,
a school trip to Chester Zoo sometime in the sixties,
Little Hoole County Primary School, Walmer Bridge, Lancashire.

The only other thing I recall
were the monkeys and the apes.
Mum and dad asked what else I'd seen …

Orange Uttans I'd replied, bold as brass.
Puzzled and confused,
I couldn't make them understand.

Out came *The How And Why Book Of Animals,*
There ! I pointed, confident,triumphant.
Oh   Orang Utans, they said.

Yes, Orange Uttans, I said
Thats how its spelt.
It must have been right – after all they were orange.

Orange Uttans and a crocodile thermometer,
the two things I remember,
everything else faded into grey, school short grey.

Still there today – in all its glue tailed glory.
Over thirty years on and I still don't know
if the reading on the back is accurate.

It may be small and broken,
it may even be useless, but that's not the point,
it's everything that goes with it.

That's why mum's kept it for so long,
along with all the other bric-a-brac we've bought,
part of our past, physical evidence.

A memory to touch.
Still there.
Always there.

Love Poem

Your eyes
Your smile
And the way you say *I love you*

The silly games
The innocent laughter
And the way you say *I love you*

The kisses from me
The kisses from you
And the way you say *I love you*

I can never run my fingers through your hair too many times

I can never tire of the hugs and the strained and tight embraces

Never bored of the songs we always sing along to

Or the books we always come back to

Watching telly from the settee is timeless with you

Holding hands by the park swings is a little piece of heaven

Sliding down the big slide never loses it's thrill

And melted ice cream is never a problem

Your eyes
Your smile
The way you say *I love you*

The silly games
The innocent laughter
The way you say *I love you*

The kisses from me
The kisses from you
The way you say *I love you ... Daddy*

Touched By The Band Of Nod

People seem to find it strange
Some may find it odd
But even after all these years
I still believe in Nod

I'm still that kid from school
Standing in the quad
Twenty five years on and more
I still singalonga Nod

I never really followed
Elton, Marc or Rod
I didn't wow 'bout Bowie
But the voice and power of Nod

The howl of Little Richard
The smile of Kenneth Dodd *
Showman, entertainer
The presence of Lord Nod

My ambition was to follow
In the path he trod
Instead of singing songs I've made
I'm writing poems about Slade
There's Jimmy, Don and then there's Dave
Not forgetting Nod

Too young to be a punk
Too old to be a mod
I was just a glam rock kid
Touched by the band of Nod

* *There's only a limited number of rhymes you know*

Something About Guitars

There's something about guitars, something ...
acoustic, electric, it doesn't really matter,
there's just something about guitars.

The shape, the feel, the sound,
the way they can hang down low,
there's just something about guitars.

Ever since I can remember
there's always been this attraction,
there's just something about guitars.

There's always been guitars ...

The plastic Beatle toy one, circa 1967,
smiling moptop face at each curved corner
that I preferred to use for machine gun noises
when shooting my sisters.

The first steel string acoustic
from cousin Alan I think,
six assorted cheesewire strings
so far from the frets
that an industrial clamp was necessary for a "G" chord.

Eko twelve string
thanks to a fifty pound loan from my Gran
and the Lancashire Evening Post small ads.
It always looked good but was never in tune.
Not that I noticed.

Hobbsy's Gibson SG shaped replica bass,
the strings not just high action
but far from parallel to the neck
although I did manage the riff from *Peaches* by The Stranglers
deng dadeng
dadenga deng deng ...

A Vox 1965 white electric
- another small ad -
I secretly hoped it would look like a Gretsch
(not knowing what a Vox looked like)
but still paid thirty five quid for something the weight of plywood

Along with the guitars, the songs ..
all based round the same five chords
three real, two made up.

If I'd been half as good as I'd wanted to be
then this wouldn't be a poem
but an album track, maybe even a single.

The trouble was, still is,
I love guitars
but I just can't play them very well.

Solos, flourishes, scales, flash ...
no chance
but chords I can do,
providing they are major and involve a maximum of three fingers.

But then again, it's the chords I love,especially electric,

the power of that one chord crashing,
reverberating and fading ... fading ... fading ...
KERCHUNNGGGGGGGG !!!!!!

I know the right pose,
just not what to play next.
That's always been the problem.

KERCHUNGG ! Guitars
KERCHUNGGGuitars
KERCHUNGGGITTAAARRRZZZZZZ...

There's always been something, just something,
there's always been something about guitars
that I'll never be able to play.

Rock Follicles

I've never had the hair,
Well, I've always had hair
I've never been that short of hair,

Even now in middle age
My hair is still there,
Still pretty much the same.

The same shade and style
That it always seems to have been
Since mum was no longer allowed near it with scissors.

But I've never had the hair,
Enough hair to really *rock*
Or *R-a-w-k*

It's never really ventured past my collar
And only just covered my ears.

It's never been permed or dyed
Or tied back in a pony tail.

It's never been wild, unkempt
Or had that dragged through a hedge backwards look.

I've never had to wear a bandanna
And it's certainly never been in my eyes.

No there's never been enough,
Never been enough
Never been enough to rock

Never been enough to rock
And I mean rock
And roll dude, good buddy

I've never really been sufficiently committed
To make that follicle statement
Of tribal style alignment

Never enough to shake wildly like Francis Rossi
Or the centre parting curtains
That makes you look like a Wacky Races Boulder Brother

Never enough to flow gracefully in perfect Harmony hairspray sheen
Like Thin Lizzy's Scott Gorham
And never enough to frizz and Afro with scarves a la Jimi Hendrix

And thankfully ... thankfully, never enough
To end up like Dave Hill, Superyob, long and straight
With silver, glitter and the absurdly curved bonkers fringe.

I Wrote The Songs

I wrote the songs
that never quite had music.
I wrote the songs
that never got rehearsed
and I wrote the songs
that ultimately never got sung.

Which is a relief for all concerned.

True, the did have melodies
but they only existed inside my head.
True, they did have verses, choruses and middle eights
but none of them I'm willing to share in their entirety.

Hackneyed phrases, obvious rhymes ...
Together, forever, whatever, I'll leave you never,
Moon, June, soon, swoon,
Tonight, alright, hold you tight
In the moonlight, outa sight,
Dressed in black, I want you back
Love you, thinking ov you,
Missing you, kissing you ...

Any subject made instantly accessible
with the proceeding words *rock and roll*
so there are *Rock 'n 'Roll Cowboys, Rock 'n 'Roll Spacemen,*
Rock 'n 'Roll Pirates, Rock 'n 'Roll Heroes,
Rock'n 'Roll Zombies and Rock'n 'Roll Vampires
usually *rockin'*
usually *rollin'*
sometimes *boppin'*
very often *strollin'*
there not being much that rhymes with *rollin'*

It's obvious what I'd been listening to
looking back at my titles...
The Boys Are Back In Town
became the not dissimilar *Back In Town with The Boys.*
Likewise *The Funky Gibbon*
transformed into the remarkably different *Funky Monkey*
(which I always thought superior as monkey and funky
actually rhymed, I mean how could they overlook that ?)
Bohemian Rhapsody was rewritten as *Hungarian Symphony*
mainly because I believed *Bohemia*
to be geographically correct.

Styles were shamelessly copied,
Slade's misspelling's accordingly adopted
U Shud No Betta
Crazee Baybee

Adolescent fantasies, writing about... love
when I couldn't even speak to females
without going seven shades of red
instead
the names of those I admired from afar
punctuate the titles with alarming regularity
and no, I'm not going to quote them here,
for fear of embarrassing them
and me
but they are there alright, loud and clear.

Embarrassing they may be,
secret, they will definitely stay
but I can't throw them away.
They remind me of who I was
and in some way
of who I now am
for if I'd never written those miles of teenage garbage
I'd never have got beyond and wrote the poems
I'm writing today
Maybe
Baybee
It's crazee
And I shud no betta

Dusting The Plants

Recently I have taken to dusting the household plants
Don't ask me what they are called,
I do not know their real names
Nor am I sufficiently enthusiastic about them
To have given them their own individual pet names.

Nevertheless, their leaves are thick and green -
But then again most leaves fit that description
Which demonstrates my knowledge on all things horticultural –
Some type of rubber plant I think –
But not real rubber obviously, I do know that much.

They are dotted around the house, here and there,
Filling shelves, tables, the landing and the mantelpiece
And recently I noticed on my wanderings between upstairs study,
Bathroom and kitchen, bedroom and living room,
That their green leaves are thick with household dust.

Man made feather dusters with feathers that have never seen a bird
Caress god's green foliage on the landing.
This is not something from the natural world
Where prairie dust and rainforest residue would be fitting
But here inside the house I am dusting the plants.

This afternoon I may take a stroll in the garden …
There is a tree in need of polishing,
Several creased flowers that could do with an iron
And the grass is somewhat grubby
So I may have to hoover the lawn.

Festival Jubilee

Greenbelt
Twenty five years of tents and mud
Twenty five years of battery recharging
Twenty five years of faith, friends and friendship

Greenbelt
Where faith has grown
Where faith has been challenged
Where art has flourished.

Changed sites over the years
But somehow always stayed something like the same.

1977 - Carey Baptist Church youth group,
Preston, M6, and me excited around Birmingham
Because I saw signs for Solihull
And thought of Slade.

A magical mix of denominations and persuasions
Culturally ecumenical
The punks, the nuns, the monks, the rockers and the goths,
The flared trousered open toed sandal with socks youth leaders
Side by side with families
Joining in one voice in the Sunday morning service
When they used to be good and had songs you actually knew.

Special place, special people

Big Eric the viking vicar
Perfect for Harry Potter's Hagrid
Flowing hair and beard
A cross between an old testament prophet, a rock band roadie
And great big cuddly teddy bear.

Simon - he's still in 1969
Jimi Hendrix's long lost paler brother
Black fringed leather jacket
Monkey boots and home made roll ups
A loud white Fender Telecaster
The most unashamed singer of Jesus songs.

Richard and The Prof
Two tenths of The Famous Potatoes
Just William, accordions, barn dances.

The hundreds of others,
Good friends everyone, family and inspiration.

Greenbelt
Where creator and creators congregate
To appreciate, liberate, invigorate
To create

A spiritual home from home
A jubilee of shared experiences
A jubilee of shared art
A jubilee of Jesus

A weekend of fun
A weekend friends
A weekend of faith
And then it's back to normality

A weekend of experiences
A weekend of excitement
A weekend of the extra-ordinary
And then it's back to mundanity

But that is what it's all about ...
Preparing to be normal
Preparing to be ordinary
Preparing for the everyday

And what we do is take the buzz,
Take the joy and inspiration.,
Take the filling of the spirit,
The wakening of the soul and mind
And hold it in our hearts
So that when we step away at last
We take the magic with us
- that pizza slice of heaven
that celestial dust blown over us

We take it back to where we are
And share it in our everyday
So that the mundane is touched by magic
And the ordinary becomes the extra-ordinary
Fuelled by the beating heart of love
That constant living pulse
From the one who joins the earth with heaven.

Greenbelt,
Just one of God's little windows.

Eternity Seems Far Too Long

Sometimes I am scared
at the concept of heaven.
It's not the being with God bit,
it's the thought of eternity,
it seems too long.

Eternity is tainted by the short comings of human nature
so I worry about boredom,
I worry about time,
I worry with a human heart
forgetting that we will be new creations
and time will be something of the past
(which won't exist anyway).

And then I look around
and think of friends and family,
those who fill our everydays,
those who we don't see as often as we should,
those we are yet to know,
those we once knew, already departed
and waiting for our arrival

And so the worry goes,
the fear disappears
because heaven will be the perfect place -
with friends and family, how could it not be?
With Jesus to meet, how could it not be?

Eternity will not be time enough
to share the joy and share the love
and eternity will finally be that state
where the jigsaw pieces fall into place
and we see the big picture as a whole.
Understanding will be complete
as horizons vanish and limits disappear
and the human soul and spirit
transforms and soars beyond our wildest, wildest dreams.

At last we will taste heaven,
the perfection of our Father's creation
and as it was meant to be
so it shall be
when we echo the words our Father said
a creation ago

It is good

And as a favourite song now sings
We re packing a suitcase to a place none of us has been
A place that has to be believed to be seen ....

Still Waiting For My Blue Peter Badge

I never got one.
I entered the competitions
But to no avail.

Having to draw my favourite footballer was one.
I drew Bobby Charlton,
Not having any pictures of the white booted Alan Ball.

Bobby running, puff cheeked and blowing
Copied from a Christmas annual,
One strand of hair blowing behind him like a pony tail.

Every Tuesday and Thursday afternoons
I would search the display board in vain
As John, Peter, Lesley and Val would point to favourites.

BBC Methodists, mum and dad let us watch each week
But thought Magpie inferior
Because it was on ITV and the presenters were scruffier.

Susan Stranks, the Brian May look alike, and the other one,
A catchier theme tune by far, it even sounded current.
Blue Peter, never really trendy but always, always there.

I got the annuals every Christmas for years
And still have them in a box somewhere
But I never got my badge.

I'm still waiting
Still waiting for that Blue Peter badge
And if I got a Crackerjack ! pencil as well...

Cutting The Long Story Short

Brevity
Is the art of

Football And Glam Rock

They said I didn't like football...
I supported Everton.

They said I didn't like music ...
I listened to Slade.

I grew up wanting to have
The passing skills of Alan Ball
And the rock and roll voice of Noddy Holder.

Instead, I grew with
The passing skills of Noddy Holder
And the rock and roll voice of Alan Ball ...

In The End It Didn t Really Matter

EVERTON 2 TOTTENHAM HOTSPUR 2 :17.8.02

I wanted to be there
I really wanted to be there
but I couldn't
and in the end it didn't really matter anyway,
I didn't really care about the match.

First game of the season -
Everton's celebration of a century in the top flight,
fifty heroes from the past to be present on the pitch.
New team, new manager,
new season, new optimism.

And I really wanted to be there.

This poem should have been about two names -
Pembridge and Radzinski,
scorers of the goals which earned a draw on a sunny day at Goodison

Instead, it's two other names that dominate the headlines.
I can only think of Holly and Jessica,
aged ten, missing ... abducted ...

Today was the day their bodies were found
Today was the day what was left of their bodies was found.

I wanted to be at the match
but at the end of the day it just didn't matter.

Bill Shankly once said that
football wasn't a matter of life or death ...
it was much more important.

Not for the first time,
he was talking rubbish.
It's only a game
and a game of football is not a matter of life and death.

I Was There

Everton 2 Arsenal 1

I was there
I was there
I was there

Lower Bullens Stand
Row N, Seat 269,
I was there

For the records
For the history books
I was there

For Arsenal's unbeaten run to end
For Wayne Rooney's debut Premiership goal
I was there

Eighty ninth minute, unstoppable,
Top left hand corner, Seaman no chance
I was there

And in that moment of the united blue roar,
The Jubilation, the joy and celebration.
We weren't just there

We were somewhere else,
Somewhere else entirely ...
Blue heaven I think

I was there.

Big Duncan Ferguson Is Not The One To Burgle Son

The house of a certain big Duncan Ferguson
Is not the one that I would choose to burgle son
Don't burgle Ferguson, I mean it stands to reason
He's in peak condition cos he's out most of the season
Out for the evening but really he's in
Maybe making tea, a sandwich with some cheese in

Big Dunc – a bit of a hunk
Big Dunc – a rebel and a punk
Six foot six of muscle and spunk
You don't want to meet him when he's violent and drunk
Once was a boozer, a boozer and a bruiser,
Playing for the blues, a winner and a loser
Break in his house – making him jump
Break in his house – you'll give him the hump
Break in his house – he'll give you a thump
Or two – pointless to resist
Big Dunc – he's got a big fist
He'll hit you so hard he'll fracture his wrist
On target more than the chances he's missed

Big Duncan – snarling like a bulldog
See his eyes popping like a bullfrog
Fists clenched, ready for a full slog

You wouldn't want to meet him in a darkened alley
Specially if you're a thieving little scally
Breaking and a entering trying to nick his tally-
Vision and his video he wouldn't seem so pally

Big Duncan could give you such a thumping
Did time for ABH or something
Don't mess about with – Big Duncan

Big Dunc – really such a nice bloke
Big Dunc – I hope that he can take a joke
If not, you won't see me for smoke

Big Duncan – not the best choice
If you're going to burgle one of the boys
In blue who plays for David Moyes

Pick someone with less intimidation
Someone who don't like all the aggravation
Not got such a bad reputation

Scott Gemmill – he's the one to break in
Don't think - he would have me quaking
Don't think - he would have me shaking
Easier to fight if I'm not mistaken
Maybe, maybe, maybe I could take him

Little Scott – he's a nice bloke
Little Scott – I hope he likes a joke
If not, you won't see me for smoke

Big Dunc's used to a bit of rough and tumble
Handy in the spat, ready for the rumble,
The argy and the bargy the push and pull and shove
Handbags at dawn and the boxing with no glove

A little bit of afters, gets their just desserts
Break into his house and you're gonna get hurt
After all this Scot's home is an English castle
Burgle Duncan Ferguson and you will get some hassle

Some of this is fact and some of this is fiction
A little bit fiction in the fact causes friction
Big Dunc – such a nice bloke
Big Dunc – I hope he likes a joke
If not, you won't see me for smoke
Big Duncan – sorry I spoke

Enjambment

enjambment
a poetical technique
whereby a stanza may finish mid

sentence
but carry on in the next
verse thereby

looking very poetical
on the printed page
a sure sign of great art

y farty pretentiousness
which personally I think
is a waste

of time and effort
and doesn't help with the
reading out loud of the p

oem as gaps
are left and
breaths are taken in the

wrong places
enjambment also has to be taught
as it is not readily accessible to

readers
not being the natural way
to read a

poem
and therefore perpetuates the
intellectual snobbery regarding adult

poetry
although it is quite pretty on the page
enjambment is really total bol

locks

Poetic Love Poem

He metaphor a drink
They had simile interests

He admired her perfect assonance
She liked his well formed ballads

They quickly became a couplet
Poetry in emotion

Unfortunately
It was just a one night stanza

The Ballad Of Johnny Clarke

Zip style method slickety slick
Bob Dylan on a stick
Mad Manc motormouth unzipped
Acid tongue Elvis Lip
Hits the target hits the mark
Who - John Cooper Clarke

Sharp edge suits back in black
Machine gun rat-a-tat-attack
Bird's nest hair and trademark shades
Twisted turn of verse and phrase
Future's bright shades are dark
Who - John Cooper Clarke

Poet L'aureat of punk
Jimmy Saville on speed and skunk
Now then now then now then now then
How's about poetry and zen
Finely honed the art of sarc
Who - John Cooper Clarke

The provocative evocative use and abuse of the syntax semtex
And the expert exponent of the explosive expletive.

The how the why the wry the dry the high velocity overdrive
The rhythm and rhyme of a talent sublime

The nicotine baritone resonates pulsates detonates reverberates
The voice of a silent generation overlooked and undervalued

Under published under rated often copied imitated
Never equalled never better

Spider limbed fag in hand
Rock and roll without a band
A deft exponent of the verbal art
The shatter proof matter of the heart
Brash bold deep and dark
Who - John Cooper Clarke
Ta very much

I Don t Wanna Be Young

I don't want trousers six feet wide
Designer training shoes
Baseball caps, gangsta raps
I don't want new tattoos
I don't want multi piercings
Or a stud right through my tongue
I'm happy in my cardigan
I don't want to be young.

I don't want a skateboard
Or Play Station Two
I don't want a mobile phone
I wouldn't know what to do
I don't want music with no tune
Or words that can't be sung
Give me Slade and Springsteen
I don't want to be young.

I don't want films without a plot
Built on special effects
Comedians who have to swear
T.V. with too much sex
But Morecambe and Wise and early nights
And a bed that is well sprung ...
I'll have those and a good night's sleep
I don't want to be young

I don't want to talk in grunts
I don't want to be bored
I don't want to hate my parents
I don't want to be ignored
I don't want that attitude
That says I'm highly strung
I want to smile instead of sneer
I don't want to be young

Family and friends that I am
Happy to be among
Having the time of my life
In the prime of my life
I don't want to be young

Time Travelling

When you move away from your village,
the place you were brought up,
the school you went to and the friends you made
the roads that connect your new life
to your old life prove that time travel exists.

For me, it's mainly the Al, the M62 and the M61.
Yes, there's a few A and B roads in there somewhere
but those are the highways that take me back to the past
and then to the present again.

They are the links between the now and the then
and as the mileometer on the car goes forwards
time reverses and memories click into ever sharper focus.
the nearer to those places in the past you get to.

Especially when things just look the same,
parents in the same house,
friends still living down the road from their parents,
the school that we went to,
the football pitch we played on,
where our dens used to be ...
it only takes a moment
and the years have flown away
like the calendar pages on a Steven Spielberg movie.

Sometimes I don't even have to close my eyes.

And in those moments
part of me wants to return to those times,
usually as the person I am now and armed with hindsight
and the knowledge that confidence brings.

Regrets, there are a few,
and even if they're mentioned it won't change a thing.

You can revisit the past
but you can never change it,
you can only alter the future.

And as the, mysteries of your life unravel,
each twist and turn, the geography of coincidence,
those turning points that punctuated experience,
those moments that defined you,
those chance happenings you once put down to luck or fate,
as all these settle into place you realise
that it is indeed the past that made you who you are
and put you in the place you are
with whoever you are with.

However great it is to go back
you can never stay for too long,
that's not where you belong
and soon it will be time
to get into the car, turn on the engine
and point the bonnet forward to the present.

For me, it's the M61, the M62 and the A1 mainly,

This is where I am now
that is where I was
I am happy with both
and it's good to play at being Doctor Who
from time to time
to time.

I Never Got My Own Back

You spat at me
Full in the face
And swore.

I twisted your arm
Because you spat in my face and swore.

Mrs Haynes looked straight at us
I waited for her to say something
About you spitting full in the face
And the words you used in class ...

Instead she told me to let go of you

You little shit
You effing, little shit
Eff off

Those were the words you used
While you spat in my face
But that's what you were
Literally.

A hanger on with the big lads
Associated with perceived power
Lapdog to the bullies
You poodle

Because of that it went no further

Me, friend of the swots, geeks and ordinary misfits,
We never fought back
Didn't know we had the power
Didn't think that we were equal
So we shied away
Away from conflict
Away from confrontation

But we had the power
We were equal
And if I knew then what I know now
I wouldn't think twice
About spitting back into your face
Twisting your arm even further
And kicking you hard in the knackers
Just for good measure

You little shit

Robert

Best friends for a term
Mostly on account of me setting you up
For the winner in football.

A good pass it was too
And you put it away beautifully,
Great goal mate.

Like all celebrations
There was fist waving, jumping
And an embrace

And that was that
The friendship was sealed
For the time being at least

I shared your taste in music,
Your sweets in class
But never your cigarettes at break

I never went behind the pool
But stayed on the tennis courts
Playing footie with a tennis ball

We never fell out,
Just sort of drifted apart over the years
Different directions, different circles ...

Friends but never best friends again
Although you did sell me your Slade elpees
- second hand, fifty pee each

And that alone
Deserves a special mention.
I've still got them ... and I still play them.

Cheers, mate.

Doug McClure, Pete Duel, Paul And Graham

Death never raised its ugly head
for major characters in serialised TV shows.
Only guest stars and bit parts died
leaving the main characters to return next week.

You always knew if someone was going to die
in Star Trek or The Virginian
because extra crew members or ranch hands
would magically appear for the fight scene.

Having been used to Doug McClure as Trampass,
seemingly eternal and indestructable
with James Drury on The Virginian
I couldn't understand,
firstly, why he was in a Foreign Legion film with Kojak,
and secondly, how he could actually be killed in battle.
I waited for him to rise Trampass like and save the day.
Even after the credits.

The first real live death I remember crying about was Pete Duel,
Hannibal Heyes to Ben Murphy's Kid Curry,
Alias Smith And Jones
(I always thought Alias was his first name ...)
He cheated death weekly on screen
but committed suicide one Christmas.
Headlines on the Nine O Clock News,
I retired to my room tearstained.
It felt strange crying over a man I'd never met
and who I only knew as a TV character, an alias at that.

Not so Paul,
He was in my class at secondary school.
Didn't come back after the Summer Holidays,
Knocked down by a car.
We didn't cry ... just stunned silence,
Never our best friend,
but inconceivable that one of us,
one so young,

someone who'd shared our English lessons
and the dinner queue
would never do so again,
And me, slightly guilty about the quip
" Boys ... and Paul" which got a laugh from the whole class.

I answered the phone
when Graham's dad told mum the news.
It hadn't hit the headlines then, but it did.
One teacher, two pupils killed
on a school trip to France,
We had cycled to school together, Graham and me,
me a sixth former, him fifth form,
united by the Everton blue.
It didn't hit me, really hit me,
until the funeral.
Seeing the coffin and the sudden knowledge
that Graham, my friend, was inside that wooden box,
forever, never coming back,
unleashed the tears I thought I'd already cried.

And so it is with passing time
it isn't just the characters,
the extras in our life, who are taken,
but the major players, the starring roles.

Everyone leaves a gap
but some gaps are bigger than others.

Stand ... And Deliver Us From ....

(For Stephen King)

This poem way well involve
vampires, ghosts, unspeakable creatures festering in shadows,
malevolent possession, alien visitations,
subhuman presence and demonic powers
so much so that you don't want to turn off the light...

There may be blood, gore, horrific unexpected deaths,
insomnia, evil, rotting corpses and dark, dark deeds ...

But this poem also involves people ...
everyday heroes, the bond of childhood friendship,
the ordinary misfits, the weak and the feeble,
the people at the centre - against the odds,
the humanity of survival - against the odds,
the togetherness that upholds and lifts the human spirit -
against the odds.

It's always about good and evil
and to truly know the worth of goodness
evil must be present and alive.

To truly know the worth of goodness
evil must be confronted.

To truly know the worth of goodness
ordinary people must make their stand
for evil to be defeated.

Light is only truly light
once there has been darkness.
Truth is only truly truth
once their has been lies.
Life is only truly life
once there has been death.

And like the books,
this poem ends with hope, humanity
and the possibility of redemption
if you just believe
and make your stand.

Master Among Mortals

I wanted to write a poem about Ken Dodd
but this cannot do him justice.
For one thing it will be too short
(and isn't it always missus?)
It should begin at seven thirty and end at one o'clock in the morning
but it will be lucky to reach the bottom of the page.

In between the verses
there will be room for a magician
with a nineteen seventies haircut
who beams beatifically from behind artificially whitened teeth
while producing farmyard wildfowl from coloured handkerchieves.
Plus there will be a pianist, resplendent in spangly diamante
who performs medleys of classic songs we don't want to remember
with a knowing wink to the audience
and is entertaining, but not necessarily for all the right reasons.

The verses themselves will be full of words like
tattifilarious, plumptiousness, discomknockeration,
happiness and tax return.

There will be references to diddy men, Jam butty mines,
tickling sticks and the flexing of the chuckle muscle missus.

Yes, it's a beautiful day,
a beautiful day to write a poem about Ken Dodd
on the back of hundred pound note,
hide it in a hole in the back garden and say
how's that for a turf accountant?

A master among mortals
Kenneth Arthur Dodd
If comedy could have one
Then Doddy would be God.

Waiting For Bruce (On A Sunny Day)

I am outside Old Trafford.
Not the football stadium
but the home of Lancashire Cricket Club.
Strangely, it is not raining.
Probably because there is no cricket today.

Tonight Bruce Springsteen and The E Street Band are playing
and no, it is not cricket

So, here I am waiting for Bruce.
Actually I am waiting for friends who are stuck in traffic.
I have a ticket for them
and cannot go in to come out.

I wonder what they're doing now
- not my friends, they are stuck in traffic -
but Bruce and the band ...

Are they even here yet?
Were they happy with the sound check
and the ambience of a cricket ground?
Would it have made a difference if it had been a baseball stadium?
Have they had afternoon tea
Has Nils tried the Eccles cakes?
Miami Steve tasted the Manchester tart?
Clarence 'Big Man' been at the parkin?
Have they done a tour of the East Lancashire countryside?
Rivington Pike is very pleasant, as is The Trough Of Bowland,
very green this time of year.
Blackpool, Southport - they may have done the seaside on their afternoon off.
I think not, but I hope if they have that they were lucky in Southport
and caught the tide when it was in, which is once in a blue moon ...
and they are rare ... even in Lancashire.

I have spent the afternoon
watching my father mow the lawn
upon which we have spent many happy hours over the last forty years or so.
Drinking tea, we passed the time talking about family and children,
like you do when you ace old enough to realise
that your parents were wiser than you'd ever given them credit.

And now I am here,
waiting outside the ground for my friends to arrive
and the show to start in earnest.

We are not allowed to take bottles or cans into the ground
so the street vendors who sold ice cold bottles of water or Coke
three hundred yards ago will no doubt come along
and pick all the full bottles off the walls
and sell them back to dehydrated punters on the way out.
At this very moment there are queues drinking in the queues
in order to get their money's worth.
No doubt there will be similar queues inside the ground
as a result of this.

Touts are touting.
Scouse touts are touting.
At the risk of stereotyping
they always seem to be Scouse touts touting.
Wherever you may go.

Not long now.
My friends will soon be here
and we will enter the gates with thanksgiving in our hearts.
Showtime beckons,
we are all waiting for Bruce
and no doubt
he is waiting for us
knowing that later on we will all,
and I mean all,
be dancing in the dark with the greatest rock and roll band in the world.

The Many Faces And Poses Of The Air Guitarist

Many faces and poses,
multiple combinations too.

Long hair is definitely helpful
so the head-titled-upwards-creating-the-waterfall-
cascading-down-the-back
or the head forward; thus bringing into play
the curtains-of-doom
or even the rapid-nod-and-spincycle-halo-of-dandruff
only add to the spectacle.

Bulging bull frog eyes and sink plunger lips
are perfect when executing the
steamhammer-powerchord-rhythm-and-riff
often accompanied by the chicken-neck-peck
and left-right-blank-owl-gaze.

Eyebrows raised, half closed eyes
and the softly exhaling *O* of the mouth
are particularly effective during lead flourishes
although expressions may attempt to mirror
emotions created by the music in question.
These may thus range from
sheer agonising pain and mental torture
to the ever so slightly constipated
to on the brink of extreme physical pleasure,
the dazed and confused state of other worldly substance
and back to the trying-to-release-trapped-flatulence-
silently-a-little-bit-at-a-time.
The Elvis lip curl and chameleon tongue are optional
although the ability to gurn is integral.

Don't forget the hands ...
rigid imaginary bar chords traversing invisible frets
or manic pink electrified maggots, blurred and rapid,
combine with a plectrum hand
that can point and wave mid solo
or mid-resonating-powerchord.

Legs ...

Can be apart, wide apart, very wide apart.
Or
the left slightly straighter with right more forward
or
one leg on the arm of the chair stroke monitor
or
the Chuck Berry waddle
or
the on-your-knees-leaning-backwards-limbo
or
the blowing up a tractor tyre with only a footpump
or
the ice down the spandex leg
or... or...

The Status Quo boogie,
the Pete Townsend windmill,
the Jimi Hendrix tooth floss ...

Endless combinations,
endless hours of fun,
all the rock and all the roll
without ever having to learn a diminished G7th chord
or the opening chords for *Smoke On The Water.*

Tempted By Tattoos

The only tattoo I ever had was at Primary school
Top infants, bottom juniors, somewhere around that time.

That's very rock'n'roll you say
Man you started early dude.

True, but I didn't have it for very long.
Mum made me wash it off before bedtime.

A penny bubbly from the comer shop
And a paper to lick and stick on my fore arm.

More of a transfer than a tattoo
But the right pirate colours of red and green..

Still, a smudged anchor is pretty cool
When you want to look a bit like Popeye The Sailor Man.

Never really tempted by *Love, Hate, Mum, Dad*
Didn't quite fancy the dotted neck and the *Cut Here*

A girlfriend's name, the logo of a favourite band,
Never committed enough to undergo the process of physical pain

The needles and the utter and complete permanence
Scared of making the wrong choices in the heat of the moment

A friend is now stuck with a *Weetabix* man and the band on his calf, *Yes*
And the name of a girl he is not married to on his arm.

Transfers — I've been tempted.
Tattoos - no.

The Bottom Line

Severe Diarrhoea
Will always lead to
A severe dire rear

The converse of this fact
Is also true I fear

The Colour Purple

I never knew purple had so many different shades
Before the vasectomy

It's different now though.

The initial interview
With a robust no-nonsense nurse, fingers like sausages,
Ushered me in and sat me down.
She shook my hand ... tightly
And at that moment I prayed it wasn't her who held the scalpel.

While never ever smiling outright
There was a hint of a smirk
As she talked about the ins and outs, the topping and tailing,
The detailed mechanics while pointing to those bits that would be going
On a chart far too large to be lifesize
- or so I hoped.

Shaving the appropriate are was problematic.

In retrospect the electric shaver was a mistake.
So was the wax.

Upon looking in the mirror
After the application of the shaving cream
It looked like one of the seven Disney dwarf's
Was resting in my lap ... Droopy perhaps.

Gillette are rightly proud of their razor blades,
Although the best a man can get
Didn't particularly inspire or give me confidence.

The physical act was akin to attempting to shave the folds
On a turkey's neck (albeit, quite a small turkey)

You always cut yourself shaving.
Those little bits of torn off toilet roll just looked silly.
The styptic pencil was mindless
And the aftershave was just thoughtless.

The needle in the gum at the dentist is bad enough.
But lying, naked from the waist down,

Legs apart, every single muscle in the body is tensed and taut
Like a trip wire ready to snap.

A few days before
I had briefly considered, in the spirit of fun,
Strategically drawing a pair of eyes,
Or the careful placement of a child's tattoo
Or perhaps getting my wife to write in biro
"Good morning cut here"
but the last thing I wanted
was a man with a laugh and shaky hand.

Two injections, one for each side,
I really wanted an anaesthetic for the anaesthetic
Instead I gritted my teeth, locked my jaw
And stared wide open eyed at the dead fly on the ceiling
While tightening every muscle another two notches,
My legs rigid and my toes pointing outward and upward,
Each toe trying to get as far away from the next one
As the needle seemed to poke up to my lungs.

Later, it seemed much later ...
The stars disappeared and I exhaled
Shakily, still tense ... very tense.

Down to the nitty gritty so to speak.
I hoped he wasn't going to go at the task willy nilly
Or beat around the bush (so to speak)

Numb from the waist down (and not for the first time either)
The operation began.
No actual feeling, just the dull and distant sensation
That a man in rubber gloves is knotting spaghetti
Where my underpants should have been
While asking about my job and where I went for my holidays
It's a bit like being at the hairdressers
But with a less attractive operative.
Split ends obviously feature somewhere along the line.

The worst part is not having the ends split
But knowing that the injection for the left side is imminent
With a needle that is now the size of a pneumatic drill
That will make the water in your eyes water
And cause the veins to stand out of your neck
So that you look like Deirdre from Coronation Street.

There is no choice
Walking like John Wayne afterwards
With half a bowl of badly shaped rotting fruit in your pants is bad enough
But I couldn't believe that purple could have so many shades and hues,
An aurora borealis of colour, even the yellows and blacks were impressive
In their rainbow like qualities and varieties.

When all was said and done and the loose ends were tied up
And I was having a cup of tea.
Then, and only then, my body decided it would be a good time to faint
Which I duly did.

If that wasn't bad enough
A few weeks later having to prepare a specimen
Proved stressful.

Trying to do so while the children are getting dressed
First thing in the morning so that the delay in taking it to the hospital isn't too long
Was not conducive to the circumstances required.
The rush, the panic,
The feeling that they may come in at any moment
Meant that I could not.
The morning post on the doormat
And shouted request as to the whereabouts of a PE kit
Served as timely interruptions.

Balancing the recepticle in the correct position
At the pivotal moment required the dexterity and hand to eye co-ordination skills
Of a juggler, contortionist and experimental scientist.

When all was said and done and the sticky situation had been dealt with
My heart sank at the quantity in the tube.
It barely covered the bottom
A sparrow could have spat more.
I wondered if there was time to add anything
Or have another go
And at the time I desperately wanted to say to my wife
"I'm struggling here, can you give me a hand"

Autumn 1976 - 30 Stitches

Fifteen years old, just
October half term holiday – potato picking week –
And on my way to Lewo's after a hard day's potato picking
To watch a James Bond film,
Early evening on my five speed racer,
Down our lane.

Quarter of a mile from our house,
Outside Harrison's Farm, where I so often played with Keith,
When *it* happened.

I don't remember *it* happening
Just the afterwards
The lights of the bus
The pain in my head and legs
Lying on the pavement
Facing back the way I'd come
The pain in my head and legs
The lights of the bus
The bus driver putting a blanket over me
Keith's dad saying *Go fetch Len, its young Paul*
The pavement, the lights,
The pain in my head and legs
Mum and dad arriving
Dad saying *By, you ve made a big dint in the pavement*
And me bleeding, lying, bleeding
While dad makes weak jokes
Waiting for the ambulance.

Thirty stitches later – in the hospital bed
Thirty stitches
You can still see the scar on the bridge of my nose
If you look carefully
Thirty stitches
And the headaches
Thirty stitches
And the pain in my right leg
Thirty stitches
Being woken every hour to check concussion
Thirty stitches

Touching my face
On the thirty stitches
Head, nose, the rough wiry spiders
Of the thirty stitches
The dried blood
The whole of my left cheek dried and crinkled
The turban bandage wrapped around the skull
And the thirty stitches.

The next day,
Not being recognised by Lewo
Even though he looked straight at me
When I spoke his name

The first time I saw myself in the mirror
And realised why I was not recognised,
I did not recognise me –
The accident fright mask,
The yellows, the blues, the purples,
The jagged stitched and crumpled paper scabs
And the thirty stitches

Found out what had happened
Hit and run
White car, overtook the bus,
Never saw me, never saw my bike lights,
I didn't stand a chance
Smashed into the back of my bike
Me – nosediving on the pavement

The bus driver saw the white of the car
I found out the car was white
When I saw the smear of white down the side of my trousers
That close

That close

Close enough to smear white
Another inch … broken leg
That close

Close enough to scoop off my shoe
And somersault it over Harrison's fence
That close

Close enough to mangle the bike
And render it a write off
That close

But not close enough for the driver to stop

But not close enough to get the registration number

Not close enough for that someone, somewhere
To be concerned enough to stop.

It's amazing how scars heal,
The skin knits, reforms
But I can still feel the chip in the bone
On the bridge of my nose
And my nose itself
- never the same again,
No longer rounded at the end but straighter
And if you look ever so closely
The right nostril just slightly higher than the left.

Hasn't changed my life,
I rarely think about it
But sometimes I wonder
Sometimes I wonder
Not about me
But the driver of the white car …

Did it change their life?
Do they ever think about it?
Did they lose sleep?
Did they have bad dreams?
Did it haunt them?
Perhaps, perhaps not.

It didn't me, but what about them?

The trouble is,
If I think too much then I may wish them guilt.
Guilt and sleepless nights

But thirty stitches – that's close
Thirty stitches – that's close

So Close And Yet So Far

The films I very nearly made
Non hit songs they never played
Books that didn't make the grade
One word or letter from success - so near and yet so far

Mathematically inept
Almost there but incorrect
Famous if I didn't get
One number out from tho being the best - I could have been a star

Trevor Island, War and Pizza,
Sloping Beauty, Wuthering Tights
Four Times A Lady, 8 Days A Week
Don't Lever Me This Way, Bogie Nights

Second To Last Of The Mohicans
Bohemian Raspberry, Stairlift to Heaven
Mama Weer All Lazee Now
Get into the Grave, Three Steps To Devon

Seven Rides For Seven Brothers
Around the World In 80 Ways
The 39 Stepladders
Monarchy In The UK

One Flew Over The Cockerel's Nest
The Lion, The Witch and The Sideboard Drawer
The Magnificent 8, the Secret 6
11th Night and The Famous 4

House Of The Rising Damp
The Frank Diary Of Anne
12 Hungry Men, Friday The 14th
That's Why The Lady Is A Tram

Sting Of The Dump, Ring Of The Lords
Harry Potter and The Gob Of Fire
Sitting On The Dock Of The Dock
Johnny B. Not Bad, Bull Of Kintyre

99 Red Baboons
Heartbreak Motel, Alehouse Rock

See You Later Escalator
Return To Brenda, Rock Around The Cock

Saturday Night's Alright for Typewriting
Just the Way You Aren't, Maggie May Not
Much Hairdo About Nothing
Jumping Jock Flush, Some Like It's Snot

Robinson Clouseau, Doctor Maybe
Gone With the Breeze, Where Beagles Dare
Mary Popout, Enter The Dragonfly
Schindler's Shopping List, Jane's Hair

24 Hours From Tesco
Sprocket Man, Can't Buy Me Glove
Wind In The Willies, Peter Pun
Baby You And Me Got A Gravy Kind Of Love

My Generator, Smoke On The Wart
Can't Get You Out Of My Shed
The Animals Of Farting Wood
Please Don't Let Me Be Misunderfed

It's Raining Menthol
The Loin Sleeps Tonight
Saturday Night Fiver, Ben Him
Tizer Feet, A Paler Shade Of White

I wanted to be remembered
I wanted my name up in lights
Nearly there, I was almost famous,
But I couldn't get it right

I wanted to join The 2 Degrees
The Jackson Six or the Five Tops
In Liverpool I formed The Booties
But eventually I had to stop

One step away from success
I've decided enough is enough
So now I'm a poet and my name is
Paul Bysshe Worsdworth Hegley Cooper Clarke Cookson Longfellow McGough

Shafaa Had Four Children

This poem was written after reading an article by Brian Reade in The Daily Mirror accompanied by a photograph during the conflict in Iraq

Shafaa
has four children,
had four children.
Now she has two.

Sarah
aged seven,
striped pyjama bottoms
101 Dalmatians top
lies on a stainless steel shelf.
She could be sleeping,
but she's not.

Shrapnel took away the back of her head
and her brother's face
so ... here they are
on a stainless steel shelf.
They could be sleeping,
But they're not.

Brother and sister could be sleeping too
but they're not.
In a coma,
they may not wake.

Sarah
aged seven forever,
will never wake
on a stainless steel shelf.
She could be sleeping,
but she's not.

Shafaa
has four children,
had four children.
Now she has two.

Shafaa says
My tears are strangled in my eyes.
They will not gush.
They are burning my soul
And will stay inside me
As a constant reminder of my anger ...

Shafaa
Has four children,
Had four children.
Now she has two.

Only just.

Footprints On The Water

Fishers of men all lost at sea
Against the gales in Galilee
Wind and water, wild and free
And footprints, footprints...
Footprints on the water.

The fist of the storm and the pummelling pain
The song and the screech and the wild refrain
Of the howling wind and the hurricane rain
And footprints, footprints...
Footprints on the water.

The boat was rocking to the left and right
Tossed like driftwood through the night
Cries of the wind and cries of fright
And footprints, footprints...
Footprints on the water.

Splintered masts, sails torn asunder
Breaking bows lurching under
To the deafening beat of the constant thunder
And footprints, footprints...
Footprints on the water.

Cracking beams on a boat that's leaking
Wailing gales like lost souls shrieking
Crashing, thrashing, groaning, creaking
And footprints, footprints...
Footprints on the water.

Whiplash spray, mountainous waves
Fathomless depths and watery graves
All seemed lost and then was saved
Footprints, footprints...
Footprints on the water.

In the tumult was released
A shaft of calm from The Prince of Peace
Just one word and the chaos ceased
Leaving footprints, footprints...
Footprints in the water.

When the storms are rough and you're hurled and tossed
And you just can't find a way across
Just have faith, all's not lost
There's footprints, footprints...
Footprints in the water.

Peter

Hi, how's it goin'?
Half an hour could never be just half an hour
It was never just popping round for a quick chat
You always had a story to tell - or two or three or more
Usually about the kids and more often than not in detail
Elaborate, exaggerated and embarrassing
And we could never get a word in edgeways anyway.

Hi, how's it goin'?
Your larger than life enthusiasm an inspiration to all you touched
The child inside of you recognised the child in all of us
One cup of tea was never ever long enough
To talk about one song, one film, one poem or one book
Time just flew and flew with you
Plus, we could never get a word in edgeways anyway.

Hi, how's it goin'?
Like a little boy in a sweet shop, wide eyed and excited
Your lists grew and grew, always open to new sounds
Drinking in each detail, memorising favourite lines
And still you couldn't sing in tune
And still you danced the same rhythm whatever the song.

Never a dull moment
When the two Guinea Pigs became twenty
You wanted to give them away in party bags.

Fan and fanatic,
Geography and favourite football teams
Celtic, Ipswich Town, Cambridge United and Sheffield Wednesday
Plus you were the only Scot I ever met to cheer on England too.
Fan, fanatic and fantastic.

So much of you to remember
So much of you in all of us

They broke the mould with you
No-one can fill the space you leave
It's cliched ... but it's true

An individual, no-one quite like you
One in a million at least
It's cliched ... but it's true

In a class of your own
Worth your weight in gold
It's cliched ... but it's true

Never a dull moment
You could talk the hind legs off a donkey
It's cliched ... but it's true

And there was no full stop
We never got to say goodbye
The book still open
Pages still to be turned

No full stop
More an extended pause
Or the long slow fade out
On a favourite song

No full stop
Just three small dots
The drifting away
So incomplete

No full stop
But the longest comma
And question mark
Your passing

No full stop
Your story unfinished
Cut short
Cruelly edited

No full stop
No satisfactory conclusion
Just three eternal dots
Dot dot dot...

Hi, how's it goin'?
Eternal optimist, your glass always half fall
The life, the heart, the soul
The legacy you leave us is the zest for life itself
And if we have a fraction of your love and warmth
Then we cannot fail to touch those round about us
And right now, all we really want
Is not to be able to get a word in edgeways
But to hear you say
Hi, how's it goin'?

The School That Time Forgot

The bell rings out for no-one
Another day begins
Pupils vee the teachers
In a war that no-one wins
Voices raised, tempers blaze
The temperature is hot
Every single day's the same
In the school that time forgot

Baseball caps and leisure wear
The new school uniform
It's nowhere near official
But everywhere it's worn
Shirts are out, buttons open,
Ties don't seem to knot
Respectable's a dirty word
In the school that time forgot

Dance beats rule the airwaves
Tomb Raider is king
Lessons all are history
They just don't mean a thing
There's always a detention
For Jason, Wayne and Scott
Trouble's never far away
In the school that time forgot

Bobby's hobby's liberating
Trapped internal wind
Noxious gases fumigating
Rooms where he has been
The stench of permanent baked beans
Is something he has got
The toxic mushroom clouds are green
In the school that time forgot.

Laura's done her make up
And laquered down her hair
Her skirts are ever shorter
You can see her underwear
The boys agree they like the view
And try to look a lot
The only look in that they get
In the school that time forgot

Lads are wearing trainers
The size of small canoes
The girls weight train their ankles
For the chunky clunky shoes
The clomp clomp of elephants
A permanent clippety clop
It's fashion. They are victims
In the school that time forgot.

Studs and rings and bolts and pins
Pierce every body part
D.I.Y. tattoos that bruise
Adorn these works of art
Heads are caked with setting gel
Sleeves are caked with snot
The situation's sticky
In the school that time forgot.

Males all move in ape like herds
Think females are inferior
The girls are more mature and know
That they are far superior
Than the grunting stooping cave boys
From the year dot
It's evolution half way through
In the school that time forgot

The macho dudes are strutting
Like peacocks acting cool
While girls their own age give themselves
To lads long since left school
Lovebite nights and laddered tights
And a lot of you know what
Some things never change
In the school that time forgot.

They can't spell virginity
But cannot wait to lose it
They've all started puberty
But don't know how to use it
Hormones rage like wildfire
Pimples start to pop
While bodies change and rearrange
In the school that time forgot.

Kieran's leering at the girls
His hands are in his kecks
The Year 10 trampoline club
Is the closest that he gets
The temperature is rising
He's bothered and he's hot
While the girls are not, and icy cool
In the school that time forgot

Darren's getting more withdrawn
His arms are always bruised
Things are getting worse
Dad's always on the booze
His mother's in the same boat
She just can't make it stop
At least he gets some respite
In the school that time forgot.

Waz is on a different plane
His chemical intake
Is not confined to cigarettes
That he inhales each break
He knows the score, he knows the draw,
Wheeler deals in pot
But nobody is buzzing
In the school that time forgot.

There are mothers hooked on valium
Fathers hooked on drink
Sisters in the family way
Big brothers in the clink
Uncles dealing drugs
What chance have they got
Hooked and stuck, their number's up
In the school that time forgot.

The writing's on the wall
The desks and chairs as well
Obscenities and football teams
Graffiti they can't spell.
Blackboards can't be written on
The lockers will not lock
Dilapidated, out of date
In the school that time forgot.

The colour of a football team
The colour of a skin
Both can be a catalyst
For trouble to begin
The wounds are always open
The blood won't start to clot
The pain and scars remain the same
In the school that time forgot.

Friction in the corridors
Violence in the yard
The weaker just get weaker
The harder get more hard
The bullies shake their rattles
Kings inside this cot
They won't own up they're not grown up
In the school that time forgot.

The staff are on the back foot
The pupils on the shelf
Their common problem seems to be
That they're not somewhere else
Unlucky for some means everyone
No-one cares a jot
No-one's learning lessons
For the school that time forgot.

Ofsted says it's failing
So tell us something new
One week then they close the door
Not leaving any clues
Blair is blurred
Hague is vague
Woodhead's lost the plot
Blunkett's really flunked it
For the schools that time forgot

New recruits have men in suits
Who haven't taught for years
Increasing jobs and workloads
Encouraging careers
Where paper pushing is a skill
To get you to the top
And children just come second
In the schools that time forgot.

Every day and time stands still
The clocks have all been stopped
Pummelled into silence
With a final tick and tock
In no man's land the second hand
Has frozen on the clock
It's ten past three forever
In the schools that time forgot.

A window to the outside world
But all the doors are locked
Ghosts alone in the phantom zone
Left on their own to rot
Then kick them when they're falling down
Ofsted's parting shot
It's ten past three forever
In the schools that time forgot

After Beezley Street by John Cooper Clarke

Last Thing At Night Poem

Out of the mundane
Let there be something,
Something of value, something creative,
Something poetic even before the day has ended.

Today I have replaced a broken toilet seat,
Mown the lawn and cut the hedges.

My football team has lost
Although my son's has won
So at least one of us is pleased.

My children are sleeping peacefully
And so is my wife.

As for me, I drowsed on the settee earlier,
mid chapter and so am not quite ready
to submit to the night just yet.

The film was good but since then
Flicking round the channels has only been partly satisfying.

Hence, I am here - at the keyboard,
Wanting to write something,
Something of worth before I switch things off.

Whether this is it, I do not know
But I do know that this is the only thing
I feel capable of writing right now.

All the other big ideas seem too much effort,
Especially at this time of night,
So this is all that's left.

I should be writing a chapter of my novel
Or poems for my new collection
But that seems like hard work.

This isn't, anyone could write this.
You should try it sometime.
Be a poet.

Everyone has at least one poem inside them
And if this poem does nothing else
Then it tells you that it wouldn't take a great deal
For your poem to be better than this one.

So go on, be a poet,
Ramble and pontificate
And don’t forget to set it out neatly.

70th Birthday Poem For Mum

70
seemed so old all those years ago
when we were the age of our children
holding hands, knee high to you

70
seemed so distant, unreachable,
impossible to think you are a pensioner
and have been for ten years

We have grown
and watched you grow
from motherhood to grandmotherhood
while never growing old

And we have watched with love and pride
as your grandchildren, our children,
love you as we have loved you,
you loving them as you loved us

Years ago you chose us
and we know now that if we had the choice
then we could choose no better

You are their hero – as you are ours,
they would not change you for the world
and neither would we

Always the same, always giving,
we would not have you change for the world
and neither would they

70
happy birthday
younger now than you have ever seemed
and long may we keep you this way

Father To Son

Until you are a father
you will not understand me,
the things I say and do
will not be fully clear
until you are a father,

Only then will you know
the heart-bursting love inside,
the pride of your achievements
and the joy of the little things
that are the big things in the end.

Only then will you feel
that you could die for your child
and only then, God forbid,
but only then will you feel that if need be
you could kill to save them too.

Until you are a father
you will not understand my anger,
my frustrations, my disappointments,
my reasons for the things I do
and my reasons for the things
I do not let you do.

Until I was a father
parts of my own father
remained a mystery, puzzles that I could not fathom.

Now that I am a father
I understand him more
and probably love him more than I have ever done before.

It somehow seems too late
but it can never be too late
and anyway, that's just the way things are,
and so I have to wait with patience
until you are a father
for then and only then
will you truly understand.

Forty Two Already

Forty two already
school days are easily recalled
and college feels positively recent

Forty two already
my 21st does not seem half my life ago,
more like ten years at the most

Forty two already
this town, south of Doncaster, has been my home
for nearly twenty years, but still I think of Lancashire- that way

So much has changed
and yet so much has somehow stayed the same...

Still interested in music, comedy, the rest
but usually when the new harks back
and sounds like the old,
trawling the past to sound like the future
but then again
I always seem to return to those first loves anyway

What made me laugh still makes me laugh
what made me sing still makes me sing
what made me want to play guitar still makes me want to play guitar
the colour of my football team, the Goodison blue
the sound of Slade, the seventies of glam and punk,
the love of Morecambe and Wise, the Goodies,
Dad's Army, Ken Dodd, The Two Ronnies,
Tommy Cooper and Les Dawson
- they just don't make 'em like they used to.

The poems and poets I read and aped,
the styles and ideas so shamelessly copied.
I've always been a poet
now it just happens to be my job as well
and those I once referred to in reverential surname terms
I'm now on first name terms with.

Still dreaming great dreams,
some already true.
Still looking to the future now
When it's only just begun

42 already
I can remember when U2 were new and unheard of,
one of my special bands, they still are.

42 already,
I sound like an old man talking about *when I were a lad,*
things were different then, kids today ...

42 already,
and while I'm not quite an old man (young for a poet *and* still alive)
my ways are becoming more set.

42 already,
so much done
so much still left to do

42 already
coincidentally, the number of lines in this poem.
See, you counted them and have found out that was a fib
and are now wondering what else I've fibbed about

And on that note ...